City
Rhythms

Written by Judy Nayer ■ *Illustrated by Clovis Martin*

MODERN CURRICULUM PRESS

MW01105179

PROJECT DIRECTOR: **Judith E. Nayer**
ART DIRECTOR: **Lisa Lopez**

Published by Modern Curriculum Press

MODERN CURRICULUM PRESS, INC.
299 Jefferson Road, Parsippany, NJ 07054
(800) 321-3106 / www.mcschool.com

Copyright © 1992 by McClanahan Book Company, Inc. All rights reserved.

This edition is published simultaneously in Canada by
Globe/Modern Curriculum Press, Toronto.

ISBN 0-8136-1110-5 (STY PK)   ISBN 0-8136-1107-5 (BK)

15 14 13 12 11   01 00 99

Oh, city kids are flipping
in the middle of the street.
They're moving to the rhythm
of this city time beat.

Oh, city kids are kicking and splish-splashing in the heat.

They're moving to the rhythm of this city time beat.

Oh, city kids are swinging and they're dangling their feet.

They're moving to the rhythm of this city time beat.

Oh, city kids are skipping and their tricks are really neat.

They're moving to the rhythm of this city time beat.

Oh, city kids are singing
and tapping with their feet.
They're moving to the rhythm
of this city time beat.

Oh, city kids are spinning
on a rink of concrete.
They're moving to the rhythm
of this city time beat.

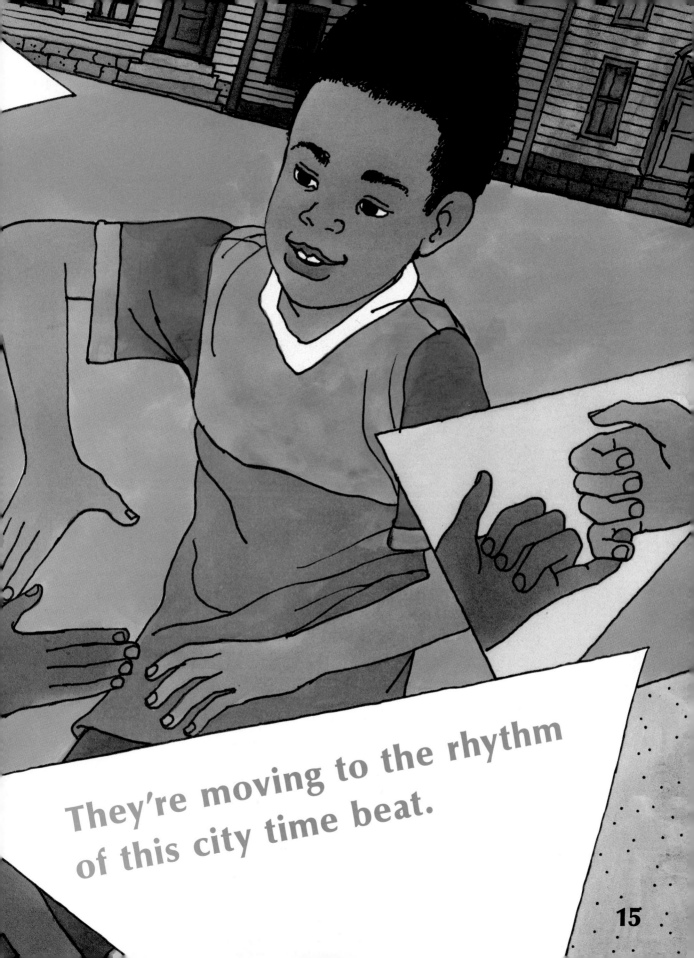

They're moving to the rhythm of this city time beat.

So, when you're in the city
and see kids you want to meet—

just move to the rhythm
of this city time beat!